GLOBAL GUARDIANS

RECYCLING, REUSING, AND CONSERVING

Devi Puri

PowerKiDS press

New York

Published in 2017 by The Rosen Publishing Group, Inc.
29 East 21st Street, New York, NY 10010

Copyright © 2017 by The Rosen Publishing Group, Inc.

All rights reserved. No part of this book may be reproduced in any form without permission in writing from the publisher, except by a reviewer.

First Edition

Editor: Theresa Morlock
Book Design: Reann Nye

Photo Credits: Cover (background), pp. 1–24 (background) jwblinn/Shutterstock.com; cover (map), pp.1–24 Buslik/Shutterstock.com; cover (top), p. 1 Imfoto/Shutterstock.com; cover (bottom) www.BillionPhotos.com/Shutterstock.com; p. 4 Volt Collection/Shutterstock.com; p. 5 Sappasit/Shutterstock.com; p. 7 Rich Carey/Shutterstock.com; p. 9 Alistair Berg/Photodisc/Shutterstock.com; p. 11 (top) Anna Omelchenko/Shutterstock.com; p. 11 (bottom) KPG Payless2/Shutterstock.com; p. 12 Kristi Dodo/Shutterstock.com; p. 13 Hurst Photo/Shutterstock.com; p. 15 (top) Yuri Turkov/Shutterstock.com; p. 15 (bottom) Alistair Berg/Iconica/Getty Images; p. 17 KPG_Payless/Shutterstock.com; p. 19 (top) Evan Lorne/Shutterstock.com; p. 19 (bottom) KaliAntye/Shutterstock.com; p. 21 alexjey/Shutterstock.com; p. 22 JGI/Tom Grill/Blend Images/Getty Images.

Cataloging-in-Publication Data

Names: Puri, Devi.
Title: Recycling, reusing, and conserving / Devi Puri.
Description: New York : PowerKids Press, 2017. | Series: Global guardians | Includes index.
Identifiers: ISBN 9781499427554 (pbk.) | ISBN 9781499429343 (library bound) | ISBN 9781508152750 (6 pack)
Subjects: LCSH: Refuse and refuse disposal–Juvenile literature. | Recycling (Waste, etc.)–Juvenile literature. | Waste minimization–Juvenile literature.
Classification: LCC TD792.P87 2017 | DDC 363.72'82–dc23

Manufactured in China

CPSIA Compliance Information: Batch #BW17PK: For Further Information contact Rosen Publishing, New York, New York at 1-800-237-9932

CONTENTS

TACKLING THE TRASH PROBLEM .. 4
THE TRASH PATH 6
USING YOUR CREATIVITY 8
CONSERVING OUR RESOURCES ...10
TO THE RECYCLING CENTER 12
THE PAPER TRAIL 14
WHERE DO ELECTRONICS GO?....16
GETTING INTO COMPOSTING 18
PARTING WITH PLASTICS....... 20
YOU CAN HELP!.............. 22
GLOSSARY................... 23
INDEX 24
WEBSITES................... 24

TACKLING THE TRASH PROBLEM

People throw away a lot of stuff. Anything you throw away is trash. Trash can be soda cans, apple cores, boxes, leftover pizza, and even old computers. As Earth's population grows, so does the amount of trash we make. Sadly, all of our trash is having a harmful effect on the planet.

The average person in the United States throws away around 4.3 pounds (2 kg) of trash a day. Over time, that adds up to a lot! It's important to look for ways to **reduce** the amount of trash you make. That will help make a cleaner and healthier world for all.

Too much trash is taking its toll on Earth. Together, we can find a way to fix the problem.

THE TRASH PATH

What happens to your trash after you throw it away? Usually big trucks come to collect the trash in your neighborhood. Often, they take it to landfills. A landfill is where waste is placed in the ground, then covered with soil. Some trash is biodegradable, which means it breaks down over time. However, trash deep in landfills breaks down very slowly. Sometimes people burn trash instead of burying it.

Landfills and burning may put **pollutants** into our air, water, and soil. Trash that ends up in the **environment** is dangerous, or unsafe, for animals. Animals, such as birds, raccoons, and dogs, can get very sick if they eat our trash.

CONSERVATION CLUES

Paper and food are biodegradable items commonly found in the trash.

There's a huge mass of trash swirling around in the Pacific Ocean. The Great Pacific Garbage Patch is made of trash that is trapped in the ocean currents. Most of the trash is not biodegradable.

USING YOUR CREATIVITY

Think about this: every time you throw something away, you're adding to the amount of trash in landfills. You can keep our world cleaner by reducing the amount of trash you make.

You can reduce trash by reusing things you already have. Decorate a used box to hold your art supplies instead of buying something new. Give old clothes to someone in need. Borrow books and movies from the library instead of buying your own. There are many ways you can help. The best part is that it doesn't cost you anything to do it!

CONSERVATION CLUES

Most communities have places to **donate** old clothes. Collect a big pile and drop it off!

It's fun to think of ways to reuse what you have, and it helps our planet.

CONSERVING OUR RESOURCES

Recycling is when you turn waste into something you can reuse, or use again. Paper, glass, and plastic can be recycled and made into new things. Making goods from recycled **materials** generally uses less **energy** than making goods from raw materials. This is important because our supply of materials is not endless.

Fossil fuels such as coal and oil are used to make some goods. Fossil fuels are nonrenewable **resources**, which means they won't last forever. Using fossil fuels can harm the environment. Scientists are figuring out better ways to use renewable resources instead of fossil fuels.

CONSERVATION CLUES

A renewable resource is one we can use over and over again, like sunlight. We will never run out of it. A nonrenewable resource, such as coal, is one that doesn't come back after we use it.

Paper, furniture, and many other goods are made from trees. Trees take in a gas called carbon dioxide and produce oxygen, which is a gas we need to live. If we cut down all of our trees, we will be in trouble.

TO THE RECYCLING CENTER

You probably use a lot of recyclable goods during the day. Plastic water bottles and soda cans can be recycled. The cans are sent to factories, where they're cut into pieces, melted down, and formed into blocks. The blocks are pressed into thin sheets that are used to make new cans. Glass bottles and jars are recyclable, too.

If you want to know if something is recyclable, look at the packaging. If you see a triangle made of arrows, it means that product is recyclable. There may be a number inside the triangle. This says what kind of material it is. This number tells the people at recycling centers how to sort the materials.

CONSERVATION CLUES

It's important to recycle plastic because most kinds don't naturally break down. They could stay in a landfill forever.

recycling symbol

The bottle you drink from at lunch may one day become a fence or a doghouse. That's cool!

THE PAPER TRAIL

Paper can almost always be recycled. After the paper is taken to a recycling center, it's separated into types. The piles of paper are washed. Special soaps remove ink, plastic, and glue. The wash also helps remove staples.

The washed paper is then mixed with water to create a slurry. A slurry is a mixture that is part liquid and part solid. Next, materials are added to the slurry to create new kinds of paper. It can become newspaper, computer paper, cardboard, or more. The slurry is spread into thin sheets. When the paper is dry, it's ready to be cut. Now we can use it!

CONSERVATION CLUES

Reducing the amount of paper you use can help the environment. Use cloth rags instead of paper towels. Wrap presents with old newspaper. Think outside the box!

paper recycling center

Most classrooms have a recycling bin for old paper. If your class doesn't have one yet, ask your teacher how you can get one.

WHERE DO ELECTRONICS GO?

People replace their cell phones, computers, and TVs all the time. Many people don't know they shouldn't throw out their electronics when they're done using them. Electronics may contain useful materials, such as copper. Sometimes, they contain unsafe **chemicals**. Common household supplies, such as paints, cleaners, and bug spray have chemicals in them, too. These chemicals are unsafe for the environment.

Schools and businesses often donate old computers and other electronics to people who need them. Most communities have a place where you can drop off your old electronics. They're then reused or recycled for parts. Electronics made from recycled materials are called "green."

CONSERVATION CLUES

Some states have laws that make it **illegal** to throw out electronics. They have to be recycled.

People throw away as much as 50 million tons (45.4 mt) of electronic waste each year.

17

GETTING INTO COMPOSTING

Organic waste is plant and animal matter such as grass clippings and eggshells. This kind of waste is biodegradable, but it takes a long time to break down when it's in a landfill. You can keep organic waste out of a landfill if you try your hand at composting.

Composting is a way to break organic matter down into a material that helps plants grow. Air, heat, water, and tiny creatures called microorganisms help the organic matter in a compost pile **decay** quickly. The end product is a rich, black material called compost. It's full of **nutrients** that plants need to grow. Adding compost to your garden's soil is a great way to help your plants grow healthy and strong.

CONSERVATION CLUES

It's easy to try composting at home. Build a compost bin and start adding organic matter. You can add apple cores, eggshells, lettuce, wood chips, grass, and more. This is called a compost pile.

compost pile

Composting is part of a closed food cycle. Leftovers from the plants you ate go into a compost pile and the compost pile produces a material that's used to grow new plants. Closed food cycles create a healthier planet for everyone.

rich, black compost

19

PARTING WITH PLASTICS

Since plastic was invented, it's become a big part of our everyday lives. Many objects, from buttons to spoons to toys, are made of plastic. Plastic is more durable and less expensive than other materials, but it's also taken a toll on the planet. Most plastics don't break down—they sit in landfills forever.

Companies are now making biodegradable plastics from plants. Some of these plastics can be composted, which is better for Earth. Some gardeners grow plants in biodegradable pots. The pots break down in the soil once they're planted. Today, stores sell biodegradable cleaning products. People are making a big effort to be kinder to our planet.

CONSERVATION CLUES

Every year, enough plastic is thrown away to circle Earth four times!

You can help Earth by using fewer plastics. Drinking from a reusable bottle is an easy way to start.

YOU CAN HELP!

Today, many people are interested in sustainability. This is the idea that we can use fewer resources and keep the environment healthy for the future. People are working to make their homes, schools, and businesses more sustainable. Single-stream recycling allows people to put all their recyclables into one bin, which makes it easier. Also, fewer bins mean fewer trucks and less energy used.

As we come up with better ways to help Earth, remember that making a difference begins with you. Recycle, reduce, and reuse at home and at school. It's fun to think of new ways to help. Conservation creates a better future for us—and for Earth.

GLOSSARY

chemical: Matter that can be mixed with other matter to create changes.

decay: To break down naturally.

donate: To give away.

energy: The power to work or to act.

environment: The natural surroundings of a person, plant, or animal.

fossil fuel: A fuel—such as coal, oil, or natural gas—that is formed in the earth from dead plants or animals.

illegal: Against the law.

material: Something from which something else can be made.

nutrient: Something taken in by a plant or animal that helps it grow and stay healthy.

pollutant: A substance that makes something unclean.

reduce: To make something smaller or less in amount.

resource: Something that can be used.

INDEX

B
biodegradable, 6, 7, 18, 20

C
cans, soda, 4, 12
carbon dioxide, 11
chemicals, 16
coal, 10
compost, 18, 19, 20

E
electronics, 16, 17
environment, 6, 10, 14, 16, 22

F
fossil fuels, 10

G
glass, 10, 12
Great Pacific Garbage Patch, 7

L
landfill, 6, 8, 12, 18, 20

N
nonrenewable resource, 10

O
oil, 10
oxygen, 11

P
Pacific Ocean, 7
paper, 6, 10, 11, 14, 15
plastic, 10, 12, 14, 20, 21
pollutants, 6

R
renewable resource, 10

S
sustainability, 22

T
trees, 11

U
United States, 4

WEBSITES

Due to the changing nature of Internet links, PowerKids Press has developed an online list of websites related to the subject of this book. This site is updated regularly. Please use this link to access the list: www.powerkidslinks.com/glob/recyc

24